MEET AL SHARPTON

MELODY'S. MIS

PowerKiDS
press.

New York

To Becky and Skip Keating

Published in 2008 by The Rosen Publishing Group, Inc.
29 East 21st Street, New York, NY 10010

First Edition

Editors: Nicole Pristash and Jennifer Way
Book Design: Julio Gil
Photo Researcher: Nicole Pristash

Photo Credits: Cover, back cover, title page, headers, pp. 5, 9, 11, 13, 15, 19 © Getty Images; p. 7 © New York Times Co./Getty Images; pp. 17, 21 © Associated Press.

Library of Congress Cataloging-in-Publication Data

Mis, Melody S.
   Meet Al Sharpton / Melody S. Mis. — 1st ed.
      p. cm. — (Civil rights leaders)
   Includes bibliographical references and index.
   Audience: Grades K–3.
   ISBN 978-1-4042-4213-5 (library binding)
   1. Sharpton, Al—Juvenile literature. 2. African Americans—Biography—Juvenile literature. 3. African American political activists—Biography—Juvenile literature. 4. African American civil rights workers—Biography—Juvenile literature. 5. African American clergy—New York (State)—New York—Biography—Juvenile literature. 6. African American politicians—New York (State)—New York—Biography—Juvenile literature. 7. New York (N.Y.)—Biography—Juvenile literature. I. Title.
   E185.97.S54M575 2008
   974.7'100496073092—dc22
   [B]
                                        2007035822

Manufactured in the United States of America

Contents

Al Sharpton is a well-known leader in the fight for equal rights. In 1991, he started a group called the National Action Network, or NAN. Its purpose is to teach people about the problems that African Americans and other **minorities** face.

Sharpton uses the National Action Network to continue the work of the civil rights movement. The civil rights movement is the name given to African Americans' struggle for equal rights. It began in the 1960s with Martin Luther King Jr.'s peaceful **protests** against **segregation** in the South. Through the National Action Network, today Sharpton talks about the unfair treatment of African Americans throughout America.

Al Sharpton is known for his strong views and powerful speeches.
He is always ready to speak out on matters he cares about.

Al Sharpton was born on October 3, 1954, in Brooklyn, New York. His family lived in a good neighborhood. At age nine, his parents ended their marriage. Sharpton and his mother had to move to a poor neighborhood where many buildings were run-down. Sharpton felt he and his neighbors could have better lives if they had more opportunities, or chances.

At age 10, Sharpton became a minister. A minister is someone who preaches, or leads church services. He traveled across the country with **gospel** singer Mahalia Jackson and preached to crowds there. Many people called him Wonder Boy because he did so much at such a young age.

Al Sharpton began preaching at Washington Temple Church, in Brooklyn, New York. He was only four years old when he started! He is seven in this picture.

From 1968 to 1972, Sharpton went to high school. He worked on the school newspaper. He also continued to preach at church on weekends.

During high school, Sharpton began working for equal rights for African Americans. He worked for Operation Breadbasket. This was a program, or plan, that helped blacks get jobs. At 14, Sharpton was made head of Operation Breadbasket's youth group in New York City. He led young people in protests and **boycotts** against companies that would not **hire** blacks. Sharpton's efforts caused many supermarkets in New York to hire African Americans.

Many large companies sold goods to blacks, but they would not hire them. Some companies would not buy goods from black-owned businesses, either. Operation Breadbasket forced these companies to change their unfair business practices.

Al Sharpton (right) and Jesse Jackson (left) have worked together many times. In 2006, they led a march, shown here, to help people who suffered through Hurricane Katrina.

In 1971, Sharpton started the National Youth Movement. It was like Operation Breadbasket because its purpose was to help blacks get jobs. The National Youth Movement protested businesses that would not hire young black people.

The National Youth Movement also worked to get companies to buy goods from businesses owned by African Americans. It also pushed large companies to let blacks buy franchises. Franchises are businesses that have been allowed to sell certain goods. Sharpton wanted blacks to have the same chances to own businesses that whites had. He wanted the African-American business community to become more powerful.

The National Youth Movement was started in 1971 to help poor children. The group raised money and worked toward keeping children away from drugs.

Al Sharpton wanted the nation to know about the unjust treatment many people in America undergo. To do this, he formed the National Action Network in 1991. Sharpton uses the network to talk about problems that African Americans and poor people face.

The National Action Network also works to get more blacks to vote in **elections**. Sharpton wants all black people to vote. He thinks if more blacks voted, the government would better address their needs. Sharpton feels their vote could give blacks the power to make their lives better.

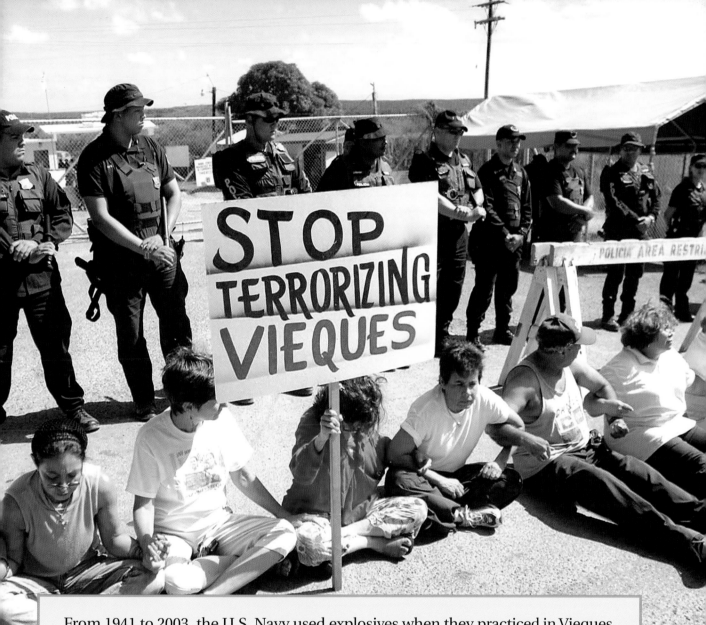

From 1941 to 2003, the U.S. Navy used explosives when they practiced in Vieques, Puerto Rico. The NAN held protests, like this one, because the explosives were unsafe.

15

Sharpton felt that many African Americans in New York were being treated unfairly. He wanted to change that, so he ran for public office in the 1980s and 1990s. He ran for the U.S. Senate and for mayor of New York City. Sharpton **campaigned** for equal jobs, housing, and schooling opportunities for blacks. He also campaigned for fair treatment by the justice system.

Sharpton did not win these races, though. His runs for office were important, however, because he got more blacks to vote. Sharpton pushed other African Americans to run for public office, as well. Many have since been elected to important government offices.

In 2004, Al Sharpton ran for president of the United States. He did not win, but his campaign brought more attention to the problems that blacks and the poor face.

During the 1980s, there were several cases in New York City in which white people killed African Americans. In some cases, the white people were not **punished**. This angered Sharpton and many others.

In 1989, an African-American boy named Yusuf Hawkins got lost in a white neighborhood called Bensonhurst. While he was there, some white boys killed him. Sharpton led marches to protest the killing. Sharpton did not want the boys to go free. He hoped the marches would force the government to punish the boys. Sharpton got his wish. The white boys were sent to prison.

Before one of the Bensonhurst marches, a white man attacked, or hurt, Sharpton with a knife. The man later said he was sorry for hurting Sharpton. In return, Sharpton helped the man get a lesser punishment.

Al Sharpton (right) honored Yusuf Hawkins at the spot where he was killed, shown here. Here, Sharpton and Yusuf's father (left) are honoring him 10 years after his death.

Al Sharpton has worked for equal rights and peace in other countries. In 1994, he was part of a group that went to South Africa. They were there to make sure the elections were fair. Nelson Mandela was running for president. He won and became the first black man to be president of South Africa. Mandela helped stop segregation in his country.

In 1994, Sharpton went to the African countries of Rwanda and Zaire. At that time, two African tribes, or groups, were fighting for control of Rwanda. Many Rwandans escaped to Zaire. Sharpton helped those who escaped by sending supplies to them in Zaire.

Al Sharpton helps people in many countries, not just in the United States. In 2003, he visited Liberia, in Africa. In this photo, he is speaking out about helping the poor there.

Since the 1980s, Sharpton has worked with music companies to hire more African Americans. He recently started a program to force singers to clean up their language. He wants people in the music business and the **media** to stop using bad words against black people. He believes these words do not show respect to black people.

Sharpton also works with large companies, such as PepsiCo and Microsoft. He wants these companies to use **advertising agencies** owned by African Americans. Because of his efforts, some large companies began to use African-American-owned advertising companies to **promote** their goods.

Al Sharpton has led many protests against the media's use of bad language.
The protest shown here took place in 2007, in New York City.

The Work Continues

Al Sharpton is one of the most talked about African-American leaders in America. His strong way of preaching makes some people angry. He continues, though, to work for equality and justice. He is always ready to lead a march against unfair treatment of blacks and other minorities.

Sharpton also works to make blacks more powerful in business and the government. He thinks this is a good way for them to control their own communities. Sharpton wants them to learn how to be successful and stand up for their rights.

Sharpton has been arrested 20 times so far in his lifetime. His arrests were reported in the news. Sharpton thinks his arrests were helpful, though. He feels his arrests let the public know about the racial problems in America.

Glossary

advertising agencies (AD-vur-tyz-ing AY-jen-seez) Businesses that try to sell something by stating it publicly.

boycotts (BOY-kots) Refusing to buy from or deal with a person, or business.

campaigned (kam-PAYND) Planned to win an election.

elections (ee-LEK-shunz) Picking someone for a position by voting for him or her.

gospel (GOS-pul) Having to do with the Bible.

hire (HYR) To get someone to work for money.

media (MEE-dee-uh) The means, such as TV and newspapers, through which facts are told to others.

minorities (my-NOR-ih-teez) Groups of people that are in some way different from the larger part of a population.

promote (pruh-MOHT) To raise attention about something.

protests (PROH-tests) Acts of disagreement.

punished (PUH-nishd) To have caused someone loss for a crime he or she has done.

segregation (seh-grih-GAY-shun) The act of keeping one group of people away from another group of people.

23

Web Sites

Due to the changing nature of Internet links, PowerKids Press has developed an online list of Web sites related to the subject of this book. This site is updated regularly. Please use this link to access the list:
www.powerkidslinks.com/crl/sharp/